THOUGHTS ON

ABRAMELIN

Thoughts

on

Abramelin

by

Ramsey Dukes

The Mouse That Spins
2019

Published by The Mouse that Spins
2019

Copyright © Lionel Snell
ISBN 0-903411-45-7

Introduction

The Abramelin Diaries by Ramsey Dukes is now available from the publisher, Aeon Books, Amazon or any bookshop.

While the book was being edited and to be published, several people expressed interest and asked questions about it, so I made a number of short videos about the work or related themes, and posted them on my YouTube channel. These videos were well received, so it occurred to me that some people might appreciate having the actual words available in print or ebook format.

So this current book is basically made up of transcripts of five past videos related to my Abramelin experience. I have edited them to remove a lot of "ums" and "youknows", and also tidied some of the wording for greater clarity. So the material is not new, but the presentation in this form and in this order might be more helpful.

If this does prove useful, I am considering making a series of booklets like this, based on other watch lists or linked themes from my YouTube channel

Ramsey Dukes

The Abramelin Diaries, Ramsey Dukes. Aeon Books, London. ISBN978-1911597193

Ramsey Dukes YouTube Channel:
https://www.youtube.com/channel/UC8-NwOu0WV5Qd_U4zOP33sw

Contents

CHAPTER ONE

What is Abramelin all about?

This was the last of the five published videos, but I begin with it because it was the one that announced the publication, so it serves as an introduction to Abramelin and its objectives.

I have been astonished at the amount of interest in this topic. When I look at the statistics for my YouTube channel, the vast majority of viewers seem to come across it when actually searching for "Abramelin" – or its variations like The Book of the Sacred Magic of Abramelin the Mage, Abramelin Operation, or whatever. Someone explained this to me by suggesting that: "Abramelin is the new ayahuasca".

It makes me wonder what people are expecting from the book. I do not want them to be disappointed.

One thing that people interested in the operation might well be looking for is advice – and there is quite a lot of advice in the book. In addition to the actual transcribed diary, I added an introduction with suggestions and recommendations for people planning to perform the operation, also some pointers to watch out for. There is also a postscript describing what happened to me after the operation.

But if you're looking for a brilliant role model, do not look here. I did it 40 years ago, and I looking back I think "God, what an idiot!" I suppose you could say that I've learned a lot since then. Even worse: if you're looking for a stunning example of magical attainment: then absolutely not.

On the other hand, if you're looking for proof that Abramelin is a total waste of time and effort, you will equally be disappointed. Because my conclusion is that, for all the struggle and things that didn't happen as hoped, it was actually one of the most valuable experiences of my whole life. It deeply influenced me over the long term and is still changing me.

Before continuing, I would give one bit of advice: six months – the time suggested for the well-known McGregor Mathers version – just wasn't long enough for me. Towards the end I really felt that I needed more time and yet the I Ching – which I was using as my advisor – told me to go back to normal life as soon as possible. So I did end aftwr six months. So I was very comforted when I came across the more recent and thoroughly researched Georg Dehn edition which claims that it should actually be eighteen months, not six. I'll come back to that topic later in this chapter.

So, what is the fascination of Abramelin? I first came across the book when I was at school, about eleven eleven years old. So imagine me, a wide-eyed kid taking my first look at the book. If you just flip through it, what first catches your eye are those pages and pages of magic squares. Those spells look like exciting stuff: you can make an army appear, you can make a house collapse, you can make a banquet appear and so on. All very thrilling: but even at eleven I knew it could not be as simple as that.

So let us for the moment stay in that childlike mode and do what we are not supposed to: start at the best bit and then read backwards. So we read back to find out what we need to do in order to be able to do these spells. Ah! The previous section explains how we have to spend almost a week working with our Holy Guardian Angel, being introduced to the good and bad spirits and learning how to use these magic squares. Okay that would be well worth it.

So we read back further to find out about this Holy Guardian Angel. We discover that it takes six months of begging your guardian angel to be manifest to you. Oh dear. For an eleven year old, six months is a very long time. But looked at from an adult point of view, it's not that onerous: actually for the first four months you are allowed to go on with your normal job, you are allowed to live with your partner and so on. So it doesn't really look so bad. At least it does not demand any of that weird stuff like the eye of a newt, or tongue of a hanged man, or whatever.

In later years, when I was preparing for it, I studied Israel Regardie views on the subject (in The Tree of Life) and he suggested that

3

those first six months are the key. (For now I'm going on talking about "six months" because that's what I did and I'll come back to the eighteen months later.) That period is the key because those are the months where you are building up the strength to be able to handle the power you aim to receive at the end. I myself had felt suspicious about those magic squares and their extraordinary promises: they look incomplete and, sure enough, Georg Dehn's research suggests that the squares in the Mathers' edition are indeed incomplete, and he has worked to fill them in from other sources.

But what I can say is that during those six months I did find myself becoming stronger and more focused, despite all my obvious failures. In particular, during the seven punishing years that followed, I learned an awful lot more. Another point about those early months of preparations is that in this operation, unlike most old grimoires, there is no protective magic circle to stand in, nor does the magician constrain the spirits into a triangle of art. Instead you are right there with them, so that your only protection lies in the strength and resistance that you have built up over those six months. That is why that part of the operation is so vital.

This does raise an interesting question: why does doing magic properly require so much strength and protection?

We live in a society which has enjoyed centuries of religious and scientific education – let's call it "rationality" for the time being – and this does not allow, or even recognise, magic. In religious terms magic goes against God's law, you are forbidden to practice it. In scientific or rationalist terms, magic goes against the laws of physics – you can't just pluck a gold coin from thin air unless it was already there. Strictly speaking, science does not forbid things in a religious manner, it rather suggests that "according to our current knowledge of physics gold coins can't just appear" – in other words science does leave the door slightly open. Magic, on the other hand, leaves it much wider open: so there is no absolute magical reason why you can't just reach into the air and pluck a gold coin, but to do so would

4

require not only the requisite skill and knowledge, it would also demand the strength to break out of our society's limitations and what we have been taught.

Actually, it's more than that. The whole of humanity, our entire evolutionary path is resistant to magic. If you go right back before humans, even before primates, a bee flying towards a flower expects to find nectar in it. Even insects are grounded in an awareness of cause and effect. So an ape might shake a tree expecting fruit to fall out of it, and a proto-human might bang two pieces of flint together, knowing that there is a good chance of getting a spark. Cause and effect is absolutely, deeply part of our entire evolution, an expectation that is deeply ingrained.

So something absolutely miraculous – like I reach out my hand and a gold coin falls into – would be breaking that ingrained sense of what can and cannot happen, and that is profoundly disturbing. You see, if that sort of thing becomes possible, it drops you into a very threatening world: if a gold coin can just materialise in my hand here, what is there to stop it from materialising a few inches away inside my brain? I would instantly be mad with pain! It might materialise inside my heart, and kill me.

A world that allowed the very basic laws that we grew up with to be broken, is suddenly a very very threatening world. So you will need enormous strength if you are going to break out of that world of deeply ingrained expectations. The entire evolution of humanity is heavily committed to not allowing real magic to happen.

In My Years of Magical Thinking, or somewhere, I described seeing a hypnotist forcing a person to witness true magic. He gave the subject a post-hypnotic suggestion that if the hypnotist snapped fingers, a certain person would become invisible; snap again, and the person would be visible again. So the person experienced real magic: he was talking to this guy and then snap, the guy vanished. Did he say "My god! He just vanished"? No, he just sort of looked away

5

without comment. Another person might say "where's John?" and get a trivial reply like "oh he went out". Snap "are you sure he went out?", "oh no, he's back now". In other words, the subjects' whole physical perception was covering over the fact something miraculous had happened.

So what I'm saying is that we must remind ourselves that, if we are going to make these spells, these stunning miraculous things happen in the way it seems to suggest in the book, then we will have to really work on ourselves. We are really having to break out of millions of years of animal and human evolution.

I loved offering analogies, so here's one to show how Abramelin relates to ordinary reality.

Let us begin with a person living in a sensible ordinary everyday world. And they have just done something very sensible: they have bought a VW Polo, a very sensible, ordinary, practical car. Then they hear a sort of rumor about someone who has got his Polo to go at 180 miles an hour. Wow! That's amazing! So they get out the Polo Owners' Manual and scour every page for information about this possibility. Nothing, Polo is clearly not allowed to go 180 miles per hour. It is impossible, the rumour was simple fantasy.

Then one day they happen on a much more esoteric tome: they have the good fortune to find the Workshop Manual – a very different sort of book, often in a great ring binder. In this manual they find instructions on how you can take the car completely to pieces, how to do things like increase the compression, change the carburetors, the timing, or whatever. All sorts of tweaks to increase the engine's power so that it might actually be able to achieve 180 miles an hour – amazing! But, reading more closely, they also learn that it would be pointless to do that before they had strengthened the clutch to handle the extra power. They'd first have to reinforce the clutch and reinforce the suspension for such speeds, and they would also have to fit high-speed tyres and better wheels to go at 180 mph. Basically, what that manual tells them is how to rebuild and strengthen the car, and how ultimately it might do the apparently forbidden thing of achieving 180 miles an hour.

Essentially, that is what this Abramelin book is telling us. As a grimoire, it's a sort of workshop manual for Life. It explains how one can dismantle one's life and expectations step by step and rebuild it in a different way. If you expect to achieve all that in just six months, you are expecting one helluva lot. Looking back after all those years, I can claim that my emotional clutch is much stronger than most people I know, and my suspension is pretty good – but I never did reach 180 mph.

The same applies to most modern magical texts: from Crowley, through Dion Fortune, WE Butler to chaos magic books – they can seem very tame, or like too much hard work, because they are doing the same thing: providing simple instructions on how to rebuild your life and the world around you to make magic more possible. In a way they have to work harder than Abramelin did because, since the Enlightenment, it has become even harder to believe in magic. It is almost as if they are taking a step even further back from the workshop manual, needing to explain the basic principles of psychic engineering and materials science before actually starting the rebuild.

What all such books do today is basically provide alternative models of the universe we live in. It can be a Kabbalistic model, like The Tree of Life, or a mythic model, such as Nordic or classical myths, or the I Ching, or whatever. These models are alternative maps of reality, ones where magic is not forbidden – even if it is difficult and rare. In these terms, the underlying secret of magical power is not so much how to make things happen but first how to allow them to happen, against those centuries of conditioning against magic.

So am I saying that modern magicians, the people who call themselves "magicians", don't really have any powers? It isn't quite like that. Take something very obvious like a money spell – everyone needs money at times. You often hear stories along these lines: "Last week I went to the market and there on a book stall was a Crowley first edition for just 19 quid! At that time I just didn't have any money. To my despair I had to leave it and walk away. But when I put my hand in my back pocket I discovered two ten pound notes notes – incredible! I rushed back and bought it". The response being "so you were really meant to have that book". That sort of happy coincidence is the stuff of most present day magic, but it is utterly unconvincing for non-magicians – for it is hardly the first time that someone had forgotten losing cash in a back pocket, then found it later.

That example shows how it is not enough simply to overcome your own deeply ingrained resistance to magic: if you want to share your magical experience with anyone else, it will multiply the resistance many times over. That means that, if you really want extraordinary miraculous things to happen, the best route is to avoid convincing others, and do it in isolation. The surest route to real magic is isolation, because secrecy allows weirder things to happen.

In my own retirement I took what the tantricists call "the way of the householder." I stayed in the same house with familiar people living around me. There were some pretty strange coincidences or interesting things that happened, but nothing that actually defied the laws of physics other than one curious event that a neighbour witnessed – but, as I would not be able to repeat what happened under laboratory conditions, it could be put down to hearsay rather than any real proof that magic can happen.

To give one example of how magical happenings can translate themselves into ordinary life: I always had problems with timing, I had some pretty heavy Saturn aspects during the operation. One day when I was really determined to get to the oratory in time, I was held up by a Spirit of Saturn. If I had been in isolation in the deepest country on my own with no one else around for six months, that spirit might have manifested directly as a mysterious dark energy pushing and holding me down and I would be forced to struggle against it to reach the Oratory. Instead I was in a home counties' suburb. So how did the spirit of Satan show itself? It suddenly turned up unannounced as a slightly sinister black haired man covered with coal dust. I said I was very busy but he said he had to deliver several bags of coal and needed me to let him in and wait while all the heavy bags of black coal – a surprising arrival in late Summer – were carried in and emptied. Then I had to to wait to sign the receipt that confirmed that the bags had indeed been delivered. So once again I was late.

Abramelin does not insist on isolation, it allows you to stay at home with your partner and even go on working. But such ordinary conditions tend to normalise the magic. As time was too short before the operation I opted for the way of the householder, rather than the way of the monk or hermit. Compared with splendid isolation, the way of the householder can sound like a soft option – even a bit of a cop-out, compared with "the real thing". Do not believe that: to stay in the family, go to work and live a fairly normal life while trying to maintain a spiritual discipline is incredibly hard. The way of the householder is a huge challenge, extremely strengthening, and absolutely not a cop-out.

So back to this question about duration: six months or eighteen? When it came to the end, I noted in the diary that I did not feel finished, I needed longer. The Georg Dehn book says it should take eighteen months, and I am pretty sure that would be needed if you want to rebuild yourself and attain serious power. I would say go into full isolation and do it for 18 months. And I strongly recommend using his corrected magic squares.

So what will you then achieve? Let us say that you can actually manifest spirits and make weird things happen as suggested. I do not think that would be impossible in the eighteen month time frame. But would you then be able to demonstrate such magic, become a public sage and convince a skeptical world?

I strongly suspect not, even given eighteen months. Instead you will now be someone who can experience impossible magical things, but will be unable to demonstrate them to other people, let alone the TV cameras or scientific community. Unfortunately our society has a word for someone that experiences weird things that no-one else can see – they are called "insane". And that is another of those barriers against practicing magic – you will be judged insane before you can convince anyone of your achievement. It sounds unfair: you do all that work to gain that power and you are just considered to be a madman.

The nearest ordinary human being to a magician with such power would be an absolute dictator. Abramelin claims that you could make a meal appear instantly, or a palace, or you can destroy a town or cause a whole Army Corps to appear. Wow, that is real power: not even a dictator could make it happen in an instant. But an absolute dictator could make a whole Army Corps appear in a wek or two, he could demand a new palace to be built in a lightning-quick time, he could destroy a town instantly with a bomb. So the only non-magical human to have anything approaching Abramelin powers would be an absolute dictator. But from what I have heard about absolute dictators, they are not the happiest of bunnies, and they do tend to go mad rather than live to a relaxed, un-paranoid old age. You see, there is something innately insane about having absolute power. If you can make everything you want happen instantly without any struggle, you will be living in a world completely created by yourself. That is like being imprisoned inside yourself – not like the rest of us for whom life at least remains an adventure, full of good and bad surprises.

So, I chose six months and the way of the householder – and half of me understands that in the eyes of many that would label me as a failure. And yet I found the Abramelin operation hugely rewarding, as I tried to explain in the book of my diary. I now think that six months is not the real Abramelin deal –it should be eighteen months – but does that mean that six months would be worthless?

No, because the whole idea of a magical retirement, when you withdraw from the world, set yourself a task and try your utmost to complete that task, is a very valuable exercise in itself. Even if you dismiss the whole magic thing.

Crowley did a magical retirement under the name John St John in just 12 intensive days and he published the resulting diary in his magazine The Equinox. The introduction to that diary is interesting because of the way he describes himself, denying that he was some wonderful sage but as "a man with all his imperfections trying blindly, yet with all his force, to control the thoughts of his mind." That really is very much what I would say about my own diary.

John St John did his retirement in 12 days. I tried it for six months and I now wish I had had a year and a half. But really it's a lifetime's work. On the other hand, even the shortest retirement is still worth attempting if performed in the right dedicated spirit and with appropriate expectations. I even recall people who recommend a long weekend retirement.

* * *

Let us now take a step back to my early exploration of The Book of Abramelin the Mage, and how I took you backwards through the book: starting with all those lovely spells, then finding out how to learn to use them by meeting all the demons, and how to get to meet your angel and so on.

What I have not yet mentioned is the very first section to the book, a Part One, where we read about the life of Abraham the Jew and his travels: how he learnt through trial and error to find this sacred magic, about his mistakes and so on. In terms of my analogy of the workshop manual, what is the role of this first section?

11

You could say that it raises the question "what's the point of getting your car to go 180 mph if you've never learned to drive a car, especally such a fast car, properly?" The messge here is that, before attempting such an operation, you would be better to live a real life and to grow up. In a very real sense I myself was not really ready in 1977. Abramelin does say that one should be over 25 to perform this magic. In some ways we mature more quickly nowadays, but in other ways modern society keeps us in a childlike state. Doing the retirement does itself provide a growing up expereince, but it helps to start in the right spirit. Either way, do not ignore the life lessons in that first part, and the messages it contains.

Another point that some people have made is about the tribulations I experienced in trying to publish this diary. Should I take them as a warning that I should not be publishing this diary? That raises a question about the fundamental drive that makes us want to be magicians: is our aim to gain power so that we may live an easier, less troubled life? Or is it to live a more interesting life? (I come back to that in a later chapter.)

At times it can feel pretty hellish, but I do find these challenges rather interesting. I still get a (maybe perverse) kick out of battling on.

CHAPTER TWO

Questions about Abramelin, secrecy and purpose

This was my first video on the subject, called Thoughts About Abramelin. It was in response to questions people asked even before I had started preparing my diaries. Questions that ultimately encouraged me to begin the project.

When I posted a video for my Lionel Snell Facebook page someone commented "I wish you would talk more about why you were slightly disappointed or disillusioned after the HGA (Holy Guardian Angel) experience. Everyone is so damn secretive about that, even when they discuss so many other ideas at length".

Secrecy is a real bugbear in magical culture. To outsiders this is what is so utterly evil about magic. The popular notion is all about hiding dark secrets and terrible deeds. I think the reason for secrecy is much simpler than that. In religious culture shared beliefs bind people together into groups, whereas magical culture is very individualistic. Even when a whole group of people are sharing a magic ritual together, the actual value of the ritual is invested more in each individual taking part – their personal experience, what it does to their life, and what it means to them personally – more than with the shared group intention. I do not deny the shared intention, it is just that the participants talk more about what they experienced and what it meant to them.

On the Internet I came across something I'd said in an interview with Phil Hine. I said that the difficulty of sharing these subjective magical experiences with non-magicians is that they can either sound exaggeratedly incredible and amazing, or else terribly banal.

An obvious example is the sort of New Age path working, where a group of people close their eyes and someone leads them to visualize an experience such as: "You are walking through a wood, down a leafy path…" and so on. When people describe their experience afterwards you get things like: "Suddenly I came across a cottage, and there was this old woman who opened the door and welcome me in…" For someone who's never done any visualization work that sounds quite amazing – that you can be sitting in a suburban room

14

and have this incredible vision of a woodland cottage. However most people who have done pathworkings know that it isn't quite like that, unless you happen to have a quite exceptional skill at visualization. Instead of being plunged into this other world, most people actually have to work at it.

I was impressed by a scene in the movie Stir of Echoes when someone was being hypnotized. As in a path working they closed their eyes and were told that they were sitting in a cinema. I cannot remember exactly what happened, but the point was that we saw the visualization through the subject's eyes and it kept having to be re-adjusted. Maybe the person pictured a cinema with rows of seats full of people, then the hypnotist says "you are all alone" and so the other people vanished. Maybe the seats were pictured covered in red velvet, then the hypnotist says "the seats are all black" and the scene quickly changes colour.

A pathworking typically begins a bit like that: you know you are actually forcing the visualization to start with. Incidentally that's why, when I actually lead a pathworking, I try to get people into a shared space early on. So I don't begin "you are walking through a forest" and then later say "you pick up a pine cone", because some people may have pictured a deciduous forest, where a pine cone would be out of place. Instead I might say: "you are walking through the dark gloom of a pine forest, you can feel the soft carpet of needles under your feet, and smell the pine resin…" That sort of sensuous detail gets people more quickly into an initial shared space.

Anyway, that's just an aside. What I'm really saying is that you might hear someone describe their experience after some New Age workshop as "suddenly the Goddess was before me. She handed me this silver chalice." It sounds absolutely incredible, when the actual experience was probably rather ephemeral and day-dreamy. This is a sort of watershed point: on one side magical experience can sound amazing, on the other side people will say "so you were really only imagining it", as if that made the whole thing worthless.

The point is that the true value of an experience like that is not so much its sensory vividness as the message it conveys. Although you may have begun by driving the vision according to instruction, it often does "come to life": so that you begin to have experiences that are not forced, surprising things emerge that you haven't consciously created. Whereas to an outsider it might still seem terribly banal, the visualization often turns up something very meaningful, even revelatory, to the person experiencing it.

That is the problem when telling other people about personal magical experiences. It is the real reason behind the culture of secrecy. It either comes across as unbelievable or utterly banal, whereas the actual truth lies between. It could be a very important experience for me, it could be one that taught me a vital lesson, but unless you enter my subjective world you will not understand its significance.

So I could say things about my Abramelin operation that make it sound astonishing – some of the weird coincidences or things that happened – and yet the real value of it could sound terribly mundane. While I was preparing for the operation, the book The Sacred Magician by William Bloom was published and it seemed to me very New Agey and pious, along the lines "today I am such a miserable worm that I have again failed to get up in time". As a proud Thelemite I was pretty snooty about all this miserable worm nonsense until, a few weeks into the operation, I too was struggling to get up in time and merely follow a simple routine properly. What an anticlimax!

In one sense you could say the whole operation was six months of disillusionment. In a more positive sense you could a describe it as a stripping away of layers of illusion. Here was I, considered to be an expert magician above the ways of the world, and yet about a month in I realized there was something in me that really did hope that I would meet an angel that could make me rich and I could buy a priceless Van Veen motorcycle. How trite and embarrassing! Another reason it would be better to keep it secret!

Stripping myself down layer by layer over six months was a disillusioning process. On the other hand I can honestly say it was the most significant and amazing year of my life in terms of what it meant to me.

People usually cut to the end and ask: "did it work?". They mean did I hit jackpot and have a wonderful vision of my angel with a shining sword, did I see spirits appearing on my doorstep and leaving their footprints in the sand. In such terms my answer is disappointing, even though I experienced a very strong sense of significance at the time. The traditional expression is "to obtain the knowledge and conversation of one's holy guardian angel", in that sense I felt that I achieved the knowledge, but not the conversation.

Above all I had a sense that it hadn't gone on long enough and so I actually kept up some of the daily meditations for quite a while after it officially ended. So I find it very interesting that a new German edition of Abramelin has been published that says it should have gone on for 18 months, not just six.

What actually happened was I went back into "normal life" – except that my life was turned upside down. It was a life-changing period. Over seven years in many small ways things happened that were analogous to what should have happened over those final seven days.

Any example I present will inevitably sound trivial to a cynic, 1 but I got a job teaching at a Steiner (Waldorf) school with 35 rather rowdy and rebellious children – this was the time of punk and Pink Floyd's "we don't want no education". As a class teacher I would be called in when they were rebelling and I had to pump myself up to sound angry so I could storm in and "put my foot down" hard. One day I suddenly realised this was just so like Abramelin's description of how you have to discipline the wicked spirits and thump the altar with your wand. Disciplinarian I was not, and yet here I was having to learn to go through the motions to get results.

After many years of never finding any job I liked, I got my first good employment in the lovely town of Winchester, I bought my own beautiful apartment in a water mill. For seven years I had been more or less living out of suitcases, so I took all my luggage in my car and arrived at this wonderful new home late at night and tired. So, should I leave my luggage in the car until tomorrow, rather than carry it up all those flights of stairs? I decided to leave it for the next day. But one of the bits of luggage was my Abramelin altar, complete with its contents untouched for years. I decided I could not leave that, so I carried it up the stairs. As I did so I felt my scalp tingling like hair standing on end. It was really creepy. Then I realized it was seven years to the day since I had completed the operation. So the next morning I set up the altar and knelt in front of it and went through my oration one more time and ended with a very strong sense of completion.

In terms of what is supposed to happen by the book, you could see that as a complete anticlimax, a rather feeble story. But for me it was hugely significant. So, in not wanting to talk about it much, it's like I want to hold onto something precious.

If you take an interest in magic, quite small things can happen that are highly meaningful. The trouble is that, in our society, there are missionaries desperate to rescue you from magic. Some are religious people who seek to rescue you from the evil of magic. Some are scientific people want to rescue from the madness and stupidity of magic. This is so important to them that they will rush to explain it all away, or tell you to abandon the path and pray.

So remember this: the magical path is very personal and individualistic. Although it is great fun to collect tales of wonder to amaze non-magicians, they are very likely to be unimpressed.

Whereas the value in a religious or scientific culture is to share experience and build community, what really matters in magic is your own personal growth.

CHAPTER THREE

Abramelin Demons – is it worth it?

This was my second video, more concerned about the difficulties experienced while resurrecting my diary and preparing it for publication.

A few months ago I was preparing to edit my Abramelin diary of 40 years ago because Aeon Books wanted to publish it. At the timet I was reading *Cave In The Snow* by Vicki McKenzie – the true story of an English woman called Diane Perry who took on the Tibetan name Tenzin Palmo and secluded herself in a remote cave 13,000 feet up in the Himalayas. She spent 12 years there, of which the last three were a strict retirement, far stricter than my Abramelin retirement. In fact she never even lay down at night, she sat in a meditation box upright all the time.

There's no way that I could really compare the physical experience of what she went through with my six months in North London suburb doing the Abramelin operation. And yet it was a fascinating read for me, because psychologically there was a lot in common between what I experienced and what she experienced. For instance: outwardly she seemed to have achieved nothing, no enlightenment. And she was even stopped from completion by police intervention. Yet she said she was never bored, it was the most valuable time of her life. I felt very much the same about my Abramelin experience.

One thing in particular struck me. A couple of times in the book it suggests that, like all journeys taken with a spiritual goal in mind, her way was strewn with difficulties and dangers. It was as if such obstacles were deliberately set in place by the heavenly powers in order to test the resolve of the spiritual seeker. I too have had that experience: a most uncanny set of obstacles being thrown in my way when trying to achieve something worthy.

I wrote something along these lines in *What I Did In My Holidays* in a short piece called *A warning to those who might consider becoming white magicians*. I gave the example of a successful city dweller who decides to throw it all in, go in for organic farming and live the simple life. Let us say these city dwellers were motivated about all the evils inflicted by human civilization on the environment and decide they will be no more part of it. So they sell their town house and set up an organic smallholding in the deepest countryside, determined to live a life of unexploitive harmony with nature. Now I suspect that deep down they somehow expect nature to thank them for this: to shower them with her abundance, to make the Sun shine on their endeavors, to make their seeds spring gratefully from the soil. In fact, too often the opposite will happen: they must expect a lousy reception, the worst weather of the century, an epidemic of mad cow disease, poxy chickens, every calamity one can imagine plus a whole crowd more. Meanwhile the factory farmer over the hill is reaping record profits and the value of city property soars.

I began that essay by giving an example of an experience I had once when I was in the deep country and needed to get a bus back home on a Sunday. But there was a bus strike, so there was a crowd of us at the bus stop getting more and more angry. Then eventually a bus did come along, absolutely stuffed full, and the conductor said "I can't take you all on board". Furious people were saying "what the hell, we've be waiting in hours!" The poor conductor replied: "I'm the person who didn't strike. I thought I owed it you people to come to this bus. But I've had nothing but abuse ever since!"

With that I drew a parallel, and the conclusion of my piece goes like this: "Indeed, anyone led by curiosity and conscience to turn from the clamor of surface reality to listen to the voices of the wind, stars and spirit must not expect reward for their dedication. Instead they must be prepared to cope with the rage of the neglected."

Now the reason this is coming up now is that, since I started to edit my Abramelin Diary, I've had so many setbacks. My Mac system, which has been so reliable for so many years, twice had to be totally rebuilt. And, within a fortnight of the second time, I had my first burglary and they took nothing except my office Mac system the one that I'd be doing the diary on.

That was just the start because, when I got out another old laptop and I went to the Apple Time Machine automatic backup to retrieve what I had lost, it said the file was corrupt. Over the months since then I spent a fortune on recovery software, and my disk has spent the last fortnight at a repair shop trying to restore files.

At the same time Cape Town, where I live, is suffering the most severe drought in known history, and my vegetable beds are shriveling up. With foresight I installed huge rainwater tanks in time to catch the last of the rain but then someone left the loos flushing when we were out, and the whole ten thousand litres washed away down the plughole. Then my oven caught fire and I had a carpal tunnel operation and one of our cats has turned diabetic so we're tied down to twice a day having to inject him with insulin…

I could list a few other things, but I don't want to sound too miserable. Basically it's a hell of a business – like the Abramelin curse is back in force.

People ask me why I do not go back to the book, banish the demons, or stop publishing my diary and burn it. Or they say I should never have done the operation in the first place.

But what about the pioneering spirit? When Sir Edmund Hilary was struggling up Mount Everest on a bad day, would you suggest he might do better to turn back and enjoy a quiet holiday in Tibet instead? In some ways I am relishing the challenge. I am determined to get this book behind me and published.

CHAPTER FOUR

On completing the edited diary – privacy and the individual

As I sent off the final proof, I reflected again on privacy and its value in our very social age, but also on how threatening it can seem to others.

I've just sent off what I hope is the final proof of the Abramelin Diaries, to be published at the end of this year 2018.

Having recently suffered a burglary, a flood, rising damp, a fire, endless computer problems, two operations and plenty financial hardship, it's very tempting to blame all those problems on Abramelin demons trying to prevent me from completing the manuscript. But actually the whole world has been having a pretty bad time recently – not just me – so I can hardly blame the whole world's political, economic and environmental crisis on wicked demons trying to stop me from publishing.

Anyway it is a relief to get it behind me.

While I was working on it, I was wondering why anyone should be interested in my struggles of 40 years ago – struggles to try to maintain a simple discipline against the background of relatively normal living conditions. Well, quite apart from the potential spiritual benefits, I think that there was real learning in simply trying to stick to a schedule of simple spiritual practice, and to keep it up for six whole months. Life does not give us many opportunities to do that.

We are constantly reminded that we live in a time of choice – a real "buyers' market". Indeed there is so much more to choose from now than in previous centuries, but it goes hand in hand with a lot of pressure to keep taking up those choices. Pressure from advertising, social media and the Internet, but also from bureaucracy and government. The one choice that has been taken from us is the choice not to keep having to make choices.

Very often I hear of people who decide they're going to commit to some practice – whether keeping fit, meditating, learning a new skill or whatever – and it fizzles out after a few weeks of months. One way some people try to keep up the discipline is to use crowd support: there are a lot of apps that encourage you not only to monitor your fitness or improve some skill every day, but also to join a community of "friends" to cheer you on, to compete or support each other. I suppose that is one way of keeping it up.

But when it comes to Abramalin, you are doing something very rare and extremely individual. That knowledge was in itself suprisingly valuable: one one hand the experience that I was doing something immensely boring and frustrating, feeling that I was an utter failure; on the other it was so different from boring and frustrating office office work or everyday failures, simply because it was something I had myself decided to do it. Unlike so much in life, it was a decision by myself and for myself – with no pressure from friends, relatives or society.

That was the real challenge: I was carving a truly individual path in a world which makes it really very difficult to do that.

In Thundersqueak, the book I wrote the year after, I mentioned the Age of Pisces, and how Pisces lies opposite the sign Virgo. Virgo represents the figure of the independent woman, the Virago if you like, who often played a sort of despised "shadow" during the Age of Pisces. People sometimes ascribe the success of the Catholic Church to the fact that it managed to integrate that shadow element by combining the Virgin with the Mother to pin her down and make her safe. But in many other cases – like the Witchcraft Trials – the independent free woman was seen as a challenge or threat to the social order.

In Thundersqueak, however, I noted that we are now moving to the

Age of Aquarius, and that the opposite sign to Aquarius is Leo – supremely the sign of the individual or "king", in contrast to Aquarius, the sign of the collective. So I suggested that the big challenge for the next two thousand years would be the individual versus society.

Just as the virago represented a sort of challenge to the Piscean world order, so might the individual play the role of the shadow, the feared opposition to Aquarius, the social and the collective.

Looking back now, I see this in two ways. One is that the more people get together on mass, the more they're inclined to yearn for a "king". Whether it takes the form of a diva, a rock star, film star or sports star, it is a figurehead that can play the role of king or queen for them. The flip side of this is that it becomes more and more dangerous to be seen as an individual, a loner, especially now with society's fears about terrorism. Whenever someone has just committed one of these school shootouts and killed lots of "innocent", the one common thing we hear afterwards is: "the killer was a bit of a loner". As if the very fact of being a loner means one is more inclined to go and shoot people.

It's become a dangerous label to bear, and of course the Abramelin operation is very much about making oneself a loner for a number of months. This type of privacy is a big challenge in our society, as I explain in my published diary.

When I first seriously started planning to do the operation, my natural instinct (having been a country boy) was to find a lonely, isolated place in the country where I could completely withdraw from society. I still think that would be a fantastic thing to do. What's more I could expect more dramatic manifestations if I did that, because it is when you are most on your own that real spiritual manifestations and magic happen more easily. As soon as you are in normal conditions with normal people around you, there is a very powerful normalizing influence, so that much less weird stuff is likely to happen. So that's what I should really do: perform it in complete isolation.

But I also realized that, in the few months I had to get ready for the operation, this would be extremely difficult – especially in a crowded country like Britain. I realized that I would be far less visible in a town, or simply staying in the suburban village I was living in at the time, on a village green in Hertfordshire. I'd be less visible there than if I found a quiet place in the woods, where sooner or later I would attract curiosity by looking like a fugitive hiding in the woods. People in the village I was in were used to seeing me around: okay, they would see me around a bit more often now, but I had already become part of the scenery. Whereas if I was in some country hideout people would become very curious – either suspecting I was up to no good or that I was an unhappy young man who needed to be cheered up, or something.

So the very first challenge was the challenge of privacy: trying to achieve a level of privacy in relatively normal circumstances. And when I now read through my diary I am appalled at the number of people that kept coming to visit. My so-called "retirement" sometimes reads like it was as a wild social life, but actually that was not quite how it was.

I went on sharing my house with a friend who knew what I was doing and knew that I wanted to be left alone. I did indeed spend a lot of time on my own. Quite apart from the actual orations in the oratory, I was trying to live in dedicated spiritual manner: trying to remain very conscious of what I was doing and why; trying to direct every action towards the operation; trying to interpret everything that happend as a message from my angel. So my house-mate was not a problem.

But of course we had many mutual friends, so people would come to visit him. Then what should I do? Should I slam the door and go away? No, because that again draws unwanted attention. Obviously if they were occult friends I would tell them I'm doing the Abramelin operation, and they would understand some of the conditions and the need to leave me alone. But it did stop them from being curious about how it was going.

For more general, non-occult friends who knew me I could get away with explaining that I was doing "a sort of meditating thing and I've got a strict routine so if you'll forgive me I won't hang around for now". I could basically get away with that. But otherwise, the more I made it clear that I wanted to be alone, the more interesting I became – and I had to find the balance to that.

So that was one of my main challenges during those six months. Other major challenges included simply getting up on time for sunrise meditation when living so far from the equator. But the challenge of balancing privacy against society and society's curiosity and suspicion would be be even worse now than back in 1977.

I wrote Thundersqueak the year after the operation and one of the things I mentioned in a recent video was that during the operation I was sort of peeling away layers of myself over six months, layers that I identified with: I am British, I am educated, I am six foot tall and so on so forth. These labels offer a sort of reward: being British I have a British passport and people in many areas hold respect for the British and it is an advantage to speak English as a native and so on. But the same labels are also traps. If anyone identifies too much with being British and invests too much importance on that label, they can easily fall victim to a politician who says things like "I'm sorry, but I'm not one of these people who's ashamed to call themselves British anymore". Statements like that win a bit of sympathy, and soon he's getting you on his side in some bogus battle.

If you understake a spiritual retreat like Abramelin, you start peeling off all those labels in the sense that you are detaching from them. It does not mean that you no longer enjoy or benefit from those labels, but you are less attached to them. There are things I like about being British, but if people start saying that because I'm British I ought to be behaving in a certain way; or if they say that as an educated person I should be thinking in a certain way – then stuff it!

Being more of an individual offers certain rewards, but it also means you're more of a threat to society.

The thing that I found was that stripping off these labels did not leave me with nothing. On the contrary, the more I detached from them, the closer I felt to the real me and my common humanity that connected me to other people. That was a big part of the value of Abramelin and yet it's a very thing which our society fears.

I compare my rather pathetic six months in a British suburb to Tenzin Palmer's three years spent thousands of feet high in the Himalayas. There she was truly isolated in a tiny cave. It was a struggle simply to reach that height with reduced oxygen and freezing temperatures. She had a really extreme retirement and yet, comparing what happened to me against what finally happened to her, the end result was not so very different. I would never claim that I achieved overall what she did, but the basic outcome was not so very different.

And yet the amazing thing was that, even in that very isolated spot, she still did not manage to complete her operation properly –

because one day a policeman struggled up to her lonely cave and told her that she was going to have to leave the country because some sort of visa or permit had expired!

The moral is that one way or another society can get you. Whether it's all the visitors that kept dropping in on me, and my having to avoid whipping up their curiosity in order to protect my privacy; or whether it's the police turning up saying "move on mate, you aren't allowed to be here" – either way there's tremendous pressure from society to defeat the individual.

I use the word "defeat" or, if we like to put it more positively, you could say it is a kindness to want to draw the individual back into society – but either way it is among the greatest struggles when you try something like Abramelin.

And yet that very struggle can also be among the most rewarding things about any sort of magical retirement.

CHAPTER FIVE

Abramelin versus Cambridge Analytica

The data leak from Facebook and the sinister role of companies that seek to mine personal data for purposes of manipulation was suddenly hot news. So I offered this piece, again opposing the individuality of magic against the pressures of society, and how magic suggests a certain dangerous freedom.

A recent news item suggested that Trump would like anyone applying for a visa to visit the United States to be required to surrender five years data on their social media activities – everything they've done on Facebook and Twitter and things like that. For many people this is rather upsetting, the thought that all that information could be in the hands of the government.

OK, most of that information the government could probably find out themselves if they wanted to – after it's all there and I can look up people's Facebook profiles and so and so forth. But it goes further than that, because there's the idea that there are special search methods which government has access to that could mine vast amounts of personal data about everyone in the country. And that is a bit scary.

To some extent I've already addressed that in my video *A Crisis in Democracy* where I pointed out that the same fear was around 40 years ago in the 1970s, and I how I had addressed such fears in my book *Thundersqueak*. But the issue become a hotter topic recently because a company called Cambridge Analytica – a company that became known a few years ago for supposedly having helped various politicians to sway public opinion by big data analysis of voters' opinions and habits – became news again. The reason being that apparently they'd had gained access to about 50 million Facebook accounts. This meant they had collected a colossal amount of searchable data on members of the public.

If it had been a question of humans having to sift through all that, I would feel sorry for them, but the fact is that Cambridge Analytica use algorithms and artificial intelligence to explore deeper, and some of those techniques are getting pretty subtle. I'm told that face recognition technology can be used to determine people's sexual orientation, even better than humans can. That is pretty amazing, and potentially scary – if sexual orientation is something that you totally identify with.

Companies like Cambridge Analytica offer behavioural change programs and are quite open about their ability to shift voting patterns and tell politicians how to manipulate the public. That too is a bit scary – because it's bad enough having commercial firms analyzing our behavior and using subtle psychology to make us buy certain things, but when it comes to actually effecting votes and swaying public opinion it all seems much more manipulative and sinister.

Going back forty years to when I did the Abramelin operation, the book does not lay down what you must be doing every single moment of every day – except in very general terms like being righteous, not doing naughty things and being vegetarian, things like that. There's a lot of freedom as to how you spend those days.

So I dedicated myself to you might call "mindfulness", trying to be very much aware all the time of the fact that I was doing this six-month operation and constantly asking myself why am I doing this, who am I and what do I want.

This approach is fundamental to a lot of magical practices, like a New Age workshop where you spend the whole weekend just asking that one question "Who am I" while working toward some sort of answer. Then, on a more shamanic level, there's the Vision Quest: where you go into nature on your own, with a question like that to search and look for signs in nature that might point you towards the answer.

So I was doing that sort of thing for six whole months, and one of the techniques I developed was written up a year later in the book *Thundersqueak*. There I described it in terms of peeling off or removing labels.

Our position in society is defined by a whole lot of labels: at that time I was 32 years old, I was an educated Englishman, I was 14 stone, I had brown hair, and and so on... I could go on forever. So this process consists of examining those labels one by one.

OK, so I was 32. For many people that would define something very important about me. But 10 years earlier I was 22, and now I'm 72 – have I totally changed into a different person? No – beneath that label there's something, a certain me which is still there. It has been there all the time. So the label "32" just doesn't seem so important anymore.

I'm an Englishman. Many people they say "Lionel, he's an Englishman" as if they had really defined me in that word. But I've been a South Africa resident for 10 years now and, if I applied to change my citizenship, would I suddenly cease to be me and become a different person? It would actually make very little difference to my self. What if I had been born in France? My parents could have gone to France and I might have grown up a French citizen. That would be a bigger difference, but I still pretty sure that deep inside I would still be very much the same.

During the Abramelin retirement I got pretty anxious when – with all that vegetarianism and fasting – I started losing weight. I was no longer 14 stone, but actually I was still the same person inside, just thinner. My hair is now white, and I am mostly bald...

So you can look at all these labels and start peeling them off. For some people it's surprising to find that what remains is actually bigger than any of the labels you've taken off. What's in the tin stays the same, and those are just labels. I called the process "removing labels" because, while you are doing it, that's what you're actually doing – taking off those labels. But of course those labels don't really go away. I'm still English. I'm still 72 and so on. But the point is you no longer attached to those labels (or should I say they are not attached to you?). In a sort of Buddhistic way you're becoming detached each time you explore those labels and realise that they aren't that important.

Now public opinion can be very rude about people doing this, this introspection. this "navel-gazing". They have a lot of negative terms to label it: individualism, selfishness, narcissism etc. The idea is – and it's quite understandable – that in doing this you're turning your back on your fellow people and becoming absorbed in yourself. But what I actually found when practicing it, is that in peeling away all those labels what you were moving towards was a form of common humanity. What is left is actually a lot of what you have in common with everyone else. It is actually those labels that separate us.

I use the term "the religious culture" in my writing, because what I describe is based on tribalism: people uniting into groups that separate them from other people: to be a Christian means you're not an atheist, nor a Moslem. Or being an atheist means you're not a Christian, and so on. Being "educated" distinguishes you from the uneducated people. These labels really are things that define what makes you different from other people. So, when you become detached from these labels, you actually find more of what your have in common with other people.

Now, being detached these labels also means that you are less likely to be manipulated by them. Some people are completely identified with and attached to being "English" – a nationalist, for example – or being American. So anything that might threaten that, or take it away, is actually very scary. Such people will do anything, they will vote for any person who promises to preserve their nationality.

For other people it might be "motherhood" as their defining label; it might be "being a man". or "being clever" or educated. The more they are attached to these labels, the more they can be manipulated – because what is also written on those labels (in small print) is what must be said to flatter you, or to reassure you, if you're not detached from them.

I mean it is really scary for some people to think that face-recognition technology might detect whether they're gay or not. But if you're not particularly attached to being gay, then it's just a label that society puts on you to try to describe your orientation or the way you feel. Is it really such a dominant issue?

This process, the magical process of looking inward and seeking the real self – in Crowley's terms it is to find your True Will – is a process of detaching from a lot of the labels that society puts on us. And society doesn't really like you doing that, because it means that society has less control over you. Politicians and the media feel less sure how to predict and control you.

Is this just me? Surely I would be an ideal subject for deep mining my buying patterns and habits, because for years I've been an avid online shopper. Even though I mostly prefer to buy in shops, I still explore and research a lot online before I go to a shop. So there's a ton of information on my habits and preferences out there, and yet the adverts that the system chooses to send me are absolute rubbish!

It's not that I've never, ever clicked on an advert out of interest, but the actual hit rate is lamentable. You know how scornful skepticks are about third-rate psychics using cold reading techniques, but I reckon that even a fourth-rate psychic, with barely a month's cold reading practice, could look me up and down and immediately sense my buying habits far more accurately than any of the algorithms that Internet advertising has so far come up with. I just don't find the adverts at all interesting, let alone convincing.

So if you are truly an individual, a free agent, this idea of big data mining personal intelligence just isn't so fearsome. They still have a hell of a long way to go before they can actually manipulate real people.

If asked to vote, or make a decision, and if I approach the issue consciously as my true self – rather than posing behind a label – the potential subtlety of my final decision would go way beyond any of those labels which are presumed to define me.

I would then be a complete human, and in that state I don't think that even Cambridge Analytica would be able to manipulate me.

If I was in any doubt about that, I could still flip a coin.

CHAPTER SIX

On manifestations

This chapter is an addition that did not feature as such in my YouTube channel

At the very start of the Abramelin operation one is required to write a vow to complete the work. To me this is very important, and I suspect that the bad reputation that the operation gained since McGregor Mathers translated it, could be because of the number of people who vowed to complete but underestimated the difficulty, failed to complete and so broke their initial vow.

So in the introduction to my diary I emphasis the need to make a realistic vow, and recognise that there are certain condition, such as police intervention or extreme danger to family or friend, that should be allowed for when you write the vow.

From that point on, the diary you keep is primarily a record of how you are sticking to that vow. In other words how thoroughly you are performing the same oration day after day

So, what happens if you have experiences that challenge your commitment, either by being disruptive or over-exciting?

For example: say you are performing the operation in isolation and are open to weird manifestations – as described in Chapter One – and on your way to oration you have a beatific vision of a deva who hails you and praises your success. This would hugely encouraging – except that it is not part of the Abramelin operation that you have vowed to complete. It is therefore a distraction. So what do you do?

You might perform a banishing ritual to remove the distraction. But then again you would be doing a magoical act that is not part of the operation you committed to. The most straightforward response would be to note the occurrence in your diary, eg: "As I went to my evening oration I met a deva... etc etc. As a consequence I was thirty minutes late for my oration."

If, however, you are taking the way of the householder, then devanic manifestations are extremely unlikely. More typically you will have a surprise visitor with some exciting news. As I explained in the first chapter, it is not appropriate just to chuck the visitor out with or without explanation. So again you will be writing in your diary: "As I went to my evening oration I met my friend… etc etc. As a consequence I was thirty minutes late for my oration."

The two statements are equivalent, and equally they are observations about how the operation is progressing. But not only do these interruptions interfere with the operation, they also impact one's self image. Meet a few impressive devas, or receive divine inspirations, and it is tempting to feel that you are being rewarded for your superb performance of the operation. Have friends drop in and delay you and you are tempted to feel that your operation is hopelessly mis-managed and you are being punished for your lamentable performance.

But both manifestations amount to the same thing: you are being distracted in a manner that makes it difficult to perform the operation properly. So, to either feel proud or ashamed of this is itself a distraction. All that matters is that you continue going to the oratory and relentlessly repeating your oration, and every deviation is recorded, however mundane.

That is why the diary, properly executed, is so dull to read. And that is why the exciting bits – when you write up your flashes of inspiration, moments of despair, weird manifestations etc – are actually a record of departures from procedure.

Writing them up, failures and all, is an exercise in non-attachment. "I was late again" is a simple statement of fact that needs to be recorded. Do so and move on. Then you will be more likely to complete the six months than if you get over-emotional about the fact and attached to your failure, or success.

Crowley indicated something similar in his *Diary of a Drug Fiend*, in the way that he handled addicts. Instead of forbidding them from taking drugs, he laid them out so people could help themselves freely. All he asked was that they made an honest record each time of when they took the drug and in what quantity. He did not exhort them to make extravagant promises, great acts of will, but simply to be honest to themselves about what they were doing.

In a similar manner, it is tempting to think that one can be the first person to perform the Abramelin operation perfectly in every detail, and to write a vow full of extravagant promises. Be warned: you will be tripped and assailed all along the way, whether by demons with pitchforks or persistent neighbours, salespeople, journalists or police.

Just note your lapses in the diary and plod on. Completion is key. What happens after those six months lies outside your control.

Lightning Source UK Ltd.
Milton Keynes UK
UKHW011154261020
372253UK00002B/308